Budget Bitch Says

Carmel McCartin

Budget Bitch Says

Published 2015 by Budget Bitch Australia

Editing & Formatting: Michael Betts
Publisher: Budget Bitch Pty Ltd
ABN 65 123 977 480
Kingston Road Thurgoona NSW 2640
www.BudgetBitch.com.au

ISBN 978-0-9875113-6-2

CONTENTS

Foreword

There are so many demands on our money; from pocket money and toy sales to downsizing the family home and learning how to be sustainable.

My reason for putting this book together is because there are so many money issues that are rarely talked about. But all of them are pertinent and many of these subjects are given little consideration when compiling a family budget.

There are many events that can change and alter the best planned budget. Oftentimes when a problem arises, we think that throwing money at it will make it go away. A little thought beforehand can make a world of difference.

Managing our money is not just a matter of earn it and spend it. We need to make sure that we can fit our lifestyle into our income for not only today but also into the future.

Despite what you may think, there is more to a budget than just recording figures. That only shows how much you have spent. It does not stop you from spending.

You may not agree with all that you read in this book, but in her true common sense style Budget Bitch says …. "If you only live for today, then how will you afford tomorrow?"

1. Where Does Your Money Go?

Have you ever wondered where your money goes? Does it seem to disappear into a black hole and even though you *know* you have not spent much, it has just vanished?

Well here is a thought – go and have a look in your cupboards. Yes that is right – look in your cupboards and look into all of them. You will probably discover that whilst your wallet is empty, your cupboards are full. You will possibly even find that some of your cupboards are over-flowing.

Let us dissect a couple of the obvious money-eating cupboards.

The bathroom cabinets: How many tubes of toothpaste are in there? How many bottles of shampoo can you find? And how many of those bottles are still half full? How many razors, bars of soap, deodorants or jars of hair products can you see? Of course the really big question is - how many rolls of toilet paper are there?

I know many people who have a “toilet paper fetish”. One girl has a whole shelf in her linen cupboard to store the rolls that cannot fit into her laundry cupboard. Another family had one hundred and four rolls when I last counted them. Now considering that they only use four rolls per week, that is a twenty-six week supply; which is six months! But they still keep buying the toilet rolls because “it was on special”.

Let me assure you – there is a special price on toilet paper *every* week. If you do not absolutely need to buy it, then you are not saving anything. In fact – you are wasting money!

Let us move on ….. Open your pantry. How many bottles of sauce are in there? How many tins of fish, fruit, or beans can you find? Can you count the packets of biscuits, cake mix, cereal, jellies and pasta? When was the last time you saw the back of the shelves? Put your hand on something from the back of the cupboard and check the use by date. Is it still current?

Your pantry might be OK, but how is your linen cupboard looking? How many towels and sheets are sitting there, still in their packaging waiting to be used? I know lots of people that constantly buy linen because they found it at a good price in a linen sale. However, I just do not understand why you would need ten sheet sets, if there are only two people living in a house!

How many cupboards are in your house? How much empty space is in those cupboards? Do you understand that it is quite OK to have empty shelves? If you feel that you cannot bear to see an empty cupboard, perhaps it would make sense to get rid of the cupboard rather than fill it with unwanted purchases.

The world economy might be looking a little gloomy – but the supermarkets are not going to close down overnight. It is not necessary to have a mini-supermarket in your house unless there is a neon sign out the front that says "Welcome to the (Insert your name here) Family Supermarket".

I once visited a family of shopaholics. They have a very large house, which also means some very large cupboards. Their pantry is almost the size of the bathroom in my house. Apart from setting up a new budget, we also spent a day doing an overhaul of their cupboards. I will not dissect what we found but suffice to say they did not need to visit the supermarket again for a month and that alone saved a thousand dollars – just from using the stuff accumulated in their cupboards first.

Sometimes the answers to our greatest financial problems are right under our very noses!

2. The Perfect Budget

One of the most asked questions of all financial people would be "what is the perfect budget?"

That is truly an excellent question and there really is no right or wrong answer. Just like the fact that we are individuals and we are all different, so too are our hopes and dreams, our lifestyles, priorities and our needs and wants.

So what might be the perfect budget for one person might not necessarily work for somebody else. Even though we might work at the same place as our friend and earn the same money each week, because our home lives and our priorities are very different, so too will our budgets be different.

There are many factors to consider in a budget: How much debt do we have? How much are our weekly, monthly and annual bills? How much income do we receive each week? What are our financial priorities? What savings would we like to put aside for the future? What will our needs be within a year? In five year's time? In a decade?

Possibly the biggest question we must ask ourselves is this: Do we have enough income to sustain the life we are leading now and into the future? Sadly for so many of us, we don't have an income problem but rather a spending problem.

Sometimes I think it is just not possible to even earn enough money to buy everything that you want!

The perfect budget is like a diamond and has many facets. It has a portion to repay our debt as soon as possible, without choking the finances. There is also a portion for day to day bills which enables us to pay these accounts on time without stress. There is also a part that puts a little aside for rainy days. So many of us have no savings and therefore have to borrow money for the times when disaster strikes. And of course, there is another section for fun - for having things we would like, things to make us feel good. That is important too. The perfect budget does not need to be too restrictive all the time.

Each part is in direct proportion to the household income and the needs of its occupants. It must be balanced so that each portion of the budget is fair to the other parts.

Of course the budget we have today will not be relevant forever. It cannot be that way. Just as we find our life continually changing, so too will our needs and wants. Our budget will have to be adjusted in accordance.

And just as our life changes, so too does our expenditure. No two months are ever the same and sometimes there are things that happen which require us to spend more money than we'd like. In a perfect world these things wouldn't occur. In a perfect budget there is enough money put aside to, at least, alleviate some of the stress without reaching for borrowed money all the time.

Finding the perfect budget for your family does not happen overnight. It takes some planning and then some test-runs to make sure the perfect mix of spending and saving are in the right proportions. It requires time and patience to get it right for you and your family.

You have to remember that it is a continual work in progress. There is no sense in starting and then giving up in less than a week. That is not giving you or your money a chance to have a financially secure future.

So how do you find this 'perfect budget'? Well, the first step is to start working on it now!

3. Where To Get Advice

Once upon a time there was a couple who had just retired from working; and upon retirement they had purchased their very first home. They had been married almost 40 years and had always rented a house but 'somebody' had told them that if they didn't spend the $130,000 superannuation payment they were going to receive as part of their retirement savings, then they would not get a pension.

This couple was so miserable living in the house that they had just bought. They owned it outright; had no mortgage to pay and they only had to put a little money aside each week to cover council rates and their insurances. So why were they not happy?

Well, they could only afford to purchase a house in an area that they did not know very well or like very much. They were too far away from all their old friends and neighbours to be able to visit as often as they were used to. And the new neighbours didn't seem to be the 'popping in' type.

Apart from that; their pension did not stretch as far as they would like and because they had spent all their retirement savings on the house, there was no money left over at the end of the week. It was not the way they had imagined their retirement to be.

After further questioning, it turned out that the 'somebody' who was giving the free financial advice was one of Jacks' (the husband) former workmates who, Jack felt, seemed to know about these things. However this workmate had no training in any other field apart from the one that he was employed in. Both men had started working together on the same day, at the same place. They were both labourers.

So because these people had received their financial advice from an unqualified 'somebody' they were actually worse off than if they had seen a professional and been given a range of the options that were available to them.

How many times have we heard stories similar to this one? We all know of people who have listened and taken advice from others who really know as little about the matter at hand as they do themselves.

If you were sick would you go to 'somebody' to make you better; or would you visit your doctor? Your financial health is just as important as your physical and psychological health and should be given the same treatment to get it into tip-top shape.

One of the hardest things in life is to admit that you "do not know how". Whether it is a matter of pride, or stubbornness, many of us seem to have a "get some help" stumbling block.

There are all sorts of people available to help you to manage your finances – whether it is on a long term or on a daily basis.

By looking in the phone book or on the Internet you will find literally hundreds of professional people who are able to assist you in organising a better financial future. You will find that you have a good choice amid Accountants, Financial Advisers, Financial Planners or Financial Counselors.

Whilst we all like to think that our personal situation is unique, have a chat to one of these professional people and you will find that they have met with many others in the same financial position as yourself.

Of course there will always be a 'somebody' who has all the answers to our financial problems, but do not forget to utilise the services of trained professionals as well. They will be worth their weight in gold – literally!

4. Do You Need A Budget?

One day a woman in her mid-forties very smugly told me that they "did not need a budget". Naturally, my curiosity was aroused because not five minutes before that statement she was complaining not only that she had to work but how much she hated it.

"So why don't you need a budget?" I asked.

Her reply was simple, "we don't have a credit card and we don't owe any money".

She then told me that she believed that people would only have a need to budget if they have debt; and she and her husband were no longer in that category.

My question about how much money they have saved in a bank account was met with a blank stare and an answer of 'Nil savings'. And what of their future, when they are no longer working? She told they have nothing apart from their respective employer funded superannuation which now amounts to about to $35,000 each. The total had been greater than that, but world economic problems had reduced their money considerably. Both of them commenced work in a by-gone era when compulsory superannuation savings in Australia did not exist for non-government workers. They had never considered a time when they would not be working.

I decided to probe a little further. How are they planning to spend their retirement? What activities would they like to enjoy? She told me that they were planning to update their car and perhaps take an overseas trip but her baffled expression made me realise that they have not thought much further than those two activities.

Have they thought about how they will manage their lifestyle whilst receiving a government pension? You see at the time of writing, in Australia the old age pension for couples is a little more than $325 each, per week. Now I cannot speak for you; but that will barely cover my household expenses.

So while this lady and her husband have worked hard to make sure they have all their debts paid out, they have not given much thought to what lies ahead when they retire. It is a common problem mainly because none of us really want to face the reality of what might happen in the future.

She readily admitted that they have frittered a lot of money away each week since they have paid off the mortgage. They easily reached their goal of being debt free before they retired but they have not given any consideration to setting any new financial goals after that.

However, they have been having a great time – fabulous holidays; luxury weekends away; dining out most nights of the week; showering their family and friends with gifts. As she explained they have really "been able to live the high-life and all of their dreams are coming true."

But then on reflection, she also realised that if the refrigerator stops working tomorrow, they do not even have the price of a new one in their bank account. That would mean going back into debt again. It was a sobering thought.

Strangely enough this is not an unusual story. There are many people in this same predicament. As a generation, the Baby Boomers have been living a fairytale; good, well-paid employment and a seemingly never ending supply of credit when they wanted it. They have been able to easily borrow and repay money from one year to the next without much thought for what happens tomorrow.

But tomorrow will come, as will the end of their working life. It happens to us all. And if we have never attempted to budget in the past, how hard will it be to do so in the future when the money is not as plentiful?

You know, for those people who have paid off their mortgage and are debt free now - even if they just saved half of their old mortgage payment each week, they would now be in a much better situation when they retire. It could mean the difference in the future as to where they can go out to dinner - either eating out in a restaurant or eating out on the back lawn.

5. Pocket Money

The "Pocket Money Issue" is something that I am constantly asked to referee when I visit families. How old the children should be when pocket money needs to be started; how often they should get pocket money; and what purpose the money serves, are just some of the points for discussion. And there is always the biggest question – how much should they get?

Lots of people tell me that kids need to learn how to manage their pocket money, first as a stepping stone to becoming financially astute in later years. That is true; although I think that financial responsibility would be a much better lesson to learn. There is no point in understanding how money markets and share portfolios work if you live on credit and do not pay your bills.

But whose responsibility is it to teach these lessons? Does it belong with the parents, the school or to somebody else?

The whole debate opens up a myriad of

questions - where does the pocket money come from? What is its purpose and what does it cover? Will the kids have a need to budget the money if their parents also buy them all the things their weekly pocket money does not cover, or even when it runs out?

Is pocket money a payment for doing household chores? If that is the case, then how much does a stay-at-home mother earn? And who pays her anyway? I am sure you have seen the many articles that have been written about how much it would cost to employ somebody to do the everyday mundane jobs that are a necessary part of living in a household.

So while it is important for young people to learn from an early age that if you want money, you have to be prepared to work for it, there has got to be a happy medium.

Surely part of what our kids need to learn is that there are certain things in this life that we must do without getting paid. Some days I would like to strangle whoever not only coined the phrase – "you get nothing for nothing", but also taught it to our kids as well.

Call me cynical but I have a mental image of dozens of young adults who have moved out of home with no clean clothes to wear, filthy floors and no clean dishes to eat from because there is nobody to pay them to do their own housework. Of course take-away food does not need dishes to eat from, but who will get paid to take out the garbage?

Should pocket money be a reward for good behaviour? What denotes a 'good' kid? And what happens to the kids who have parents that complain about how bad they have been lately? Do they still get their allowance? In which case one might then ask if the money is being used as a bribe for good or appropriate behaviour.

Of course a lot of the pocket money questions that I have to answer are about how to fit these payments into the family budget. Sadly I see many households where the pocket money portion is larger than the weekly allowance for utilities and therefore it is no wonder that some families are struggling to pay their bills on time.

Whilst every household and family is

different, some of the potential pocket money problems can be alleviated by all parties discussing the family budget and where the allowances can fit within that.

A good rule of thumb is - if the children are too young to understand or participate in a family budget discussion, then they just might be too young to receive an allowance of their own.

The answers to this common dilemma lie within our individual concepts and values of money management.

6. Can You Afford A Helicopter?

Nowadays I find it quite common to hear talk about adult children, aged well into their twenties and often their thirties, who are still living in the family home with their parents. It is not a new topic. Rumblings have been heard since 2006 and indeed there are a few different groups who have heard me speak on the subject.

"Helicopter Kids" is a term used to describe these young and not-so-young adults who live with their parents. Bernard Salt, one of Australia's leading demographic commentators, coined the term in his book, *The Big Picture,* as a name for the off-spring who "perennially hover about the family home refusing to fully move out and establish their own household". [1]

There are some family therapists of the opinion that if you treat your twenty-two year old like a twelve year old, by doing their washing and cooking for them and also paying their bills, then you are depriving them of the opportunity to learn crucial skills for living independently.

To my mind there are two parties at fault; the kids who do not really want to grow up and be responsible adults, and the parents who are not letting them do so. In both cases, it is quite often an unconscious action or reaction by all parties involved.

Of course money is an area that can become a stumbling block for parental pride. Sadly I know many parents who readily admit they have never said 'no' to their children, regardless of their age. While most would agree that it is wonderful knowing that your kids want to live with you, admitting that it puts a large financial strain on the household is a real challenge. Which parents sit down and discuss their personal finances with the adult members of their family?

When investments and superannuation do not perform as well as many would like, many parents who were aiming for an early retirement, are quite often scrambling to find the funds to support themselves once they leave the workforce. Those of their offspring who have enjoyed a life totally funded (thus far) by "The Bank of Mum and Dad" could be forgiven for feeling that their world is having its' own personal financial crisis.

Most parents want to give their kids a good financial start in life. There is nothing wrong with that idea. Allowing them to live in the family home means that an education debt can be repaid, or a rental bond or home deposit can be saved. And let us admit it to ourselves – the way things are looking sometimes, this just might end up being the only financial assistance we will be able to give them.

But while giving them reduced rent (or no rent) is one thing, contributing towards their living costs is quite another issue. How many times have we heard the story of the adult son who ate the chicken from the fridge (in one snack-fest sitting) that was supposed to be for the family dinner? Or the daughter who ran up a phone bill equivalent to the monthly mortgage repayment?

It is time to be sensible – they do not need to pay off their parents' mortgage, but they do need to be responsible for paying their own way. That is just part of being a responsible adult.

Families can alleviate the stress that surrounds this complex issue by sitting down and openly discussing the costs of running a household which is now full of adults. All parties need the opportunity to negotiate a reasonable amount for board that honestly reflects the full costs of additional food and utility bills.

If you can no longer afford the cost of a helicopter and the whole subject is too daunting to organise, maybe it is time to ask an independent person to help your family plan a strategy that will work for you.

Remember! Your kids are now adults and they need to learn this valuable lesson – before they leave home!

[1] Bernard Salt, *The Big Picture: Life, Work and Relationships in the 21st Century*, Hardie Grant Books, Prahran, Victoria, 2006, p64

7. Shopping From Habit

If the Macquarie Dictionary defines the word *habit* as *"a disposition or tendency, constantly shown, to act in a certain way"* [2] then you will realise that in lots of ways we are all creatures of habit in many areas of our life.

But have you ever stopped and really thought about your own practices? Why you do what you do when you do it?

Take for example the regular grocery shopping expedition. How many of us go to the same place, on the same day of the week at roughly the same time? And then once we are there, we take a trolley and start at the same aisle and go the same route to get roughly the same purchases as the time before?

Of course that probably means we also spend the same amount of money each time.

Do you not just hate it when the supermarket decides to shake things up a bit and change the aisles around? No longer is the toothpaste in the same place and the bread has changed places with the cereal. It can be downright confusing and certainly makes this chore less than enjoyable.

But have you ever stopped to wonder why they do this? Do you think it is all about getting you to actually see what they have for sale, in the hope that you will buy more? Do you think that they are also trying to shake up a few habits?

Have you ever noticed how the things they would really like you to buy are at your eye-level? And the things that they would like your kids to pester you to buy are at the junior-shoppers eye-level. It is all a part of their marketing strategy, but if you look above or below these levels you are sure to find lots of other bargain priced goods.

For so many of us, the whole hunting and gathering of food for our families is based on habit. And rather than trying to change too many habits all in one day let me ask this question – do you really have to buy your food supplies at the same time every week?

Now lots of times I hear the cry – "there will

be nothing in the house to eat". But I am yet to find a house where the cupboards really do look as bare as that infamous Mrs. Hubbard from that old nursery tale. There is always something in there – even if it is just an old tin of chick-peas left over from the school fete.

I met with a well-organised family who has a weekly menu and shopping list prepared every week. Not only does this cut down the impulse buying at the supermarket but it also means that there is not a lot of stuff lurking in the pantry that will never be eaten. Well, that is the theory anyway. However, even in this well managed kitchen we were able to find enough cans and tins to make dinner for a couple of nights.

So if you moved your grocery shopping to a different day and a different time what do you think might happen? Would a great hole appear in the freezer cabinet and suck you right inside, never to be seen again?

If you were to go a day later each time, do you suppose you would think about what you needed to buy?

Supermarket shopping does not have to be a deep and meaningful experience. But if we give a little more thought to the whys' and wherefores' of what we are spending our money on, I am sure we will find that the whole excursion has just become a huge habit that is eating into our budgets.

[2] "habit". *MacquarieDictionary.com.au* 2015 http://www.macquariedictionary.com.au (6 October 2015)

8. How To Make Your Budget Work

Once you have made a start and organised a budget, the toughest part is to stick to it. And you have to stick to it for more than a couple of weeks if you really want to make some successful changes to your finances.

Think about it – this is one of the greatest challenges you will ever have to face. Why? Because you will be changing some habits than you never thought you had. Plus you will also have to "row against the tide" of peer pressure.

What habits? I can almost hear the amazement in your voice. Well for starters, there is the habit of swiping your plastic card without thinking about how much you have just spent. Then of course there is the habit of "just buying it anyway" because you would really like it as a treat, or buying it just because it seems cheap.

Throw in a couple of shopping sprees for

things you just want rather than really need, add a few take-away meals each week as well as a sprinkling of nights-out and you have the makings of a short-lived budget.

Apart from the changes in the way you spend your money, you also have to cope with well-meaning family and friends who sabotage your plans to get your finances back in shape. They do not mean to, but you have to admit: it is not in their interests for you to blaze a trail in the savings account department. It might make them feel guilty about their own financial shape.

How to stay strong with all these adverse outside influences? One of the first things you can do is to write your savings goal on a piece of paper. Then stick that paper where you will see it several times every day. This will remind you what you are working towards, and why you are doing it.

Next, make a promise to yourself that for the next three weeks you'll only go to the supermarket if you have a shopping list prepared. Make a pact with yourself that you will not have any unplanned shopping trips, and also make the decision to buy only the things that are on your list.

Do some planning in advance; weekly menus, family activities, and ways to spend your time without spending loads of money. Getting your whole household involved will make things easier over the coming weeks.

Focus on the positive aspects of what you are doing rather than the negative things that you perceive you might be missing out on. It takes three weeks to change a habit, so do not expect to wake up on the second morning and have everything under control.

Get yourself a coach, or mentor; someone to give you encouragement when things get a little tough in the first few weeks. Spend time with positive people, and others who are going down the same path as you. Sharing the load is always beneficial.

Making your budget work is a lot like losing weight. It is not about trimming some fat for a while then falling off the wagon until the next time you want a guilt trip, or everything is too tight again. It is a lifestyle change and once you realise that you will move forward in leaps and bounds.

Of course, the only way to make your budget work is to actually get started and if you do not know how, or what to do next – find somebody that can help you.

There is no excuse for saying you do not know how!

9. Have We Forgotten How To Be Frugal?

Sometimes it seems that every time you open a paper or turn on a TV the news is filled with gloomy stories of economic downturns and it would appear that the whole world is still reeling from financial turmoil. The stories of bankruptcy and mounting debt are truly horrific.

We all feel the pinch in some way and sometimes our incomes do not seem to stretch as far as they once did. There seems to be continual demands on our money each week.

Why has this happened?

Is it because for so long we have lived in a world of "have it now and pay for it later" that, amongst other things, we have forgotten how to be frugal?

What is 'frugal'? (Believe it or not, there are some people who have never even heard the word)

Well, the Macquarie Dictionary defines *frugal* as *'economical in use or expenditure; prudently saving or sparing'* [3]. So let us just break that down into everyday terms.

We have forgotten how to save water. How many loads of washing do you do each week? Is it really necessary to do that many? Do our clothes really get that dirty in a couple of hours – or have we just forgotten how to hang them up again. Is this something we can teach the younger members of our family?

We have forgotten how to save electricity. Are there lights on constantly in your house? What appliances are running all day, inside or outside your house? Is it absolutely necessary to have them on all the time? How many times a day do we boil the kettle and not use the water? I will put my hand up and admit to that one. I often get distracted and wander off whilst making a cuppa.

We have forgotten how to save on fuel. When was the last time you walked anywhere? How many times this week did you take the car, or drive to somewhere close enough for you, or your family, to walk to?

We have forgotten how to cook. How many take-away or pre-packaged meals have you had this week? How many times have you taken your lunch to work? How many times have you eaten out?

It takes time to cook, and time equals money (we all know this), but if you are spending all your money to avoid cooking (by getting others to prepare your food) – then the food budget may be a little out of kilter.

We have surely forgotten how to do things for ourselves. How much do you pay to have your lawns mowed or your pool cleaned and maintained? How often do you pay for a house cleaner, or somebody to iron your clothes?

We may think that we have to pay for these things because we are too busy to do them ourselves. We have become time-poor. But really, the more housework we out-source, the longer we will need to work so that we can afford the money to pay to have the chores done for us.

Why would you pay $15ph to have your ironing done when you are only earning around $20ph yourself?

There are so many ways we can be frugal without dramatically changing our lifestyle. These days there is no social stigma attached to the word frugal. It all comes back to that 'B' word (budget) and making sure that your lifestyle fits the income you earn.

While we cannot change the world situation we can make things better in our own world, for ourselves and our families.

[3] "frugal". *MacquarieDictionary.com.au* 2015 http://www.macquariedictionary.com.au (6 October 2015)

10. What Does Saving Mean?

We seem to have forgotten what the word saving means.

The Macquarie Dictionary defines the word *save* as *'to avoid the spending, consumption, or waste of'* and *saving* (plural) as *'sums of money saved by economy and laid away'* [4].

So if that is the case, then why do we hear people say "I bought such-and-such for X amount of dollars and saved X amount of money".

Now forgive if I am wrong but (to my mind) that is not saving, that is actually spending. I suppose it might not be spending as much as you could have - but it is still spending!

From what I understand from the definition of the word, the only way you could actually save money in this instance would be to put the amount that you have supposedly saved into a bank account. Now that would be saving! But does anybody ever do this?

So then I need to ask this question – "How can you save money by spending money?" To me it does not make sense!

Perhaps people are getting confused with the old adage – "you have to spend money to make money". That is a common term used in business and I am not going to delve into the whys' and wherefores' of that right now. (You should have the money to spend before you actually spend it, but that is another topic for another book).

Buying stuff to store in a cupboard is certainly not making money. There are many people who purchase items in the hope that one day they will be worth a lot more money. But what about antiques and collectibles you ask? Good question! Go and look at the stuff you bought. Is it going to appreciate in value in your lifetime? Is it a rare and valuable piece that is hard to find?

If not, then your argument is not as strong as the advertising that sucked you into believing that by spending money on a purchase, you will actually save money.

How many times have you bought something just because it was cheap? How many times have you bought something that was on 'special', regardless of whether you needed it or not? It is easy to convince ourselves that we need it when we see something at a perceived bargain price.

Think about the times you have been drawn into a store that had a rack of clothing on display with a sign offering two items for the price of one. How brainwashed have we become that we can so often believe that we will be saving money if we make such a purchase? Ask yourself if you really need two of these items? And if the answer is no, then why not only buy one? You are really not saving any money by buying two.

In our minds it is easier to justify spending the money if we think we are getting it at a "never to be repeated" price. But unless we truly need the product that we are purchasing, then the only thing we are saving is an excuse for the next time there is an argument about the amount of money we are spending.

Take a walk through any shopping mall and count the "savings" signs. They are everywhere and it is so tempting to think that we just might purchase something for less than full price. But it is still not saving money.

Buying things when they are on sale is the way to spend less money. It has absolutely nothing to do with saving money.

The only signs that really have the save money message in perspective are the ones outside the bank that say – "open a savings account today".

[4] "save", "saving". *MacquarieDictionary.com.au* 2015 http://www.macquariedictionary.com.au (6 October 2015)

11. Toy Sales

Have you noticed that there are an enormous amount of toy sales that occur in the middle of the year? It is no accident. In Australia Toy Sales are designed to entice winter shoppers out from their warm houses and into the stores. They advertise large discounts on toys so that parents can begin to get ready for Christmas.

In some cases they offer a free lay-by arrangement which means that the shopper can store the toys at the shop while they pay them off. What a great idea!

As a kid, I often wondered where Santa stored all the goodies that so obviously could not fit inside his sleigh.

But one day when initiating a discussion on the topic, I threw in the thought that "toy sales mean that parents can spend huge sums of money so that their kids can impress people they don't even know or like".

It was an interesting debate. One argument was that some parents like the lay-by arrangements, as it gave them a chance to buy big-ticket items that they would not ordinarily be able to afford in December. At that thought, I could not help myself; I had to float the idea that perhaps they could put a little money aside each week to pay for the festivities at Christmas.

Of course, the savings idea was then counteracted by mums and dads telling me that they might not be able to afford everything on the Santa List if they did it that way. Whoa! If all the wants on the wish-list are being fulfilled every year, then I am moving in!

Using the lay-by system is a good idea. There are no interest costs and the penalty for not making the payments is that the goods are not released till they are paid for. But once again we are conditioning ourselves to constantly paying off things we would like to have. It means that we are always living in debt.

And I need to ask this question – what happens if you lay-by something now that your child has gone off by Christmas? What happens if they have changed their mind and do not want those goods?

The discussion was not all one-sided. There were people who agreed that perhaps the children of today have high expectations of material possessions because constant advertising and peer pressure point them in that direction. These were the parents who freely admitted that they would never be able to afford everything that their kids asked for. And that is the reality that every generation of parents must face. Even with a million dollars to spend, I doubt that every wish could be fulfilled.

Sometimes I wonder if converting a child's bedroom to the equivalent of a mini toy store is just to satisfy our own desires. So I have to ask – How many times have you bought a gift for your child because it is something that you have always desired?

One father sadly admitted that the model train set that he had insisted on buying for his son was really to complete his own childhood dream and it was only ever used when they were together. It seems that in this instance, spending time together was more valuable than spending money.

It concerns me greatly that maybe we are teaching our children to copy our love of consumerism and I am curious to know if future generations will also have a "keep up with the Joneses" mentality.

As I have said many times before – the greatest gift you can give to anyone is the gift of time.

So the next time that you line up in the queue at the toy sales, ask yourself this – "If I gave my child a choice between this wonderful toy and a full day of doing things together, which would they choose?"

I know what my answer would be.

12. Do We Really Need Up-sizing?

Have you noticed just how much we live in a society that is obsessed with up-sizing everything?

With phrases like - "get more for your money" and "bigger bang for your buck" we are becoming conditioned to believing that big is beautiful.

Seriously, just take a good look around you and you will see what I mean. Up-sizing seems to be everywhere and if you are not sure where to start looking then take a trip to your shopping mall for a tea break or perhaps lunch.

Recently I met with friends for coffee at a cafe. There were three coffee sizes available – small, medium and large. I love good coffee and had intended to order a large one until I actually noticed the sizes of each container. The small was what I would call large; and the large one looked like it held half a bucket. I could not have drunk it all in one sitting. I ordered a small sized one and my friends were amazed. It seems very few people order one that size.

Then I looked at the muffins. The price was good, but the huge size meant that half of it would be wasted. I could not fit all of that muffin and a coffee into me, and besides our break was not long enough for the time it would take to eat the whole thing.

Supermarkets have also increased the size of many goods. Have you ever noticed how much bigger some of the items have become? With the size of many cereal boxes nowadays, it would take over a month for two people to get through it all. That is, if their breakfast appetites have not been up-sized to match.

And therein lies a large part of the problem with Australia's sky-rocketing obesity levels. Food packaging and meal sizes have grown and our waistlines are keeping up with the pace.

There are people who complain about spending more and more at the supermarket but I challenge them to look in their pantry. You might be spending the same amount or more each week, but you are possibly eating more because of up-sizing.

Of course nobody likes to waste good food. We eat it instead.

Whatever happened to the saying – "less is more"?

Have you noticed that we have up-sized our vehicles? Have a look in the carparks and see how many big vehicles are parked there. It appears to be normal to drive an SUV or a people mover if you have more than two persons in your family. Maybe the reason is because none of us fit inside the smaller cars anymore. Of course up-sizing your car means up-sizing the amount of fuel you need.

And have you seen how the humble delivery vans are now being made an equivalent size to a mini-bus? It makes me wonder, if you have to get a special licence to drive a mini-bus, why the drivers of these bigger vehicles are not made to do the same.

Even the family home has been up-sized. We are living in bigger houses, but our families are now smaller. Living areas are bigger. So too are garages and sheds. Unfortunately many times we do not have the time to enjoy this extra space, because we have up-sized our social activities and are never at home.

Our wages are bigger than any generation that have gone before. Our debt levels are also bigger than in the past, but our savings accounts are smaller. We have also up-sized the opportunities for funding our retirement, but how many of us take full advantage of them?

TV's, toys, lifestyles, the list goes on .....

Whilst looking back at history when houses were small and families were large, one cannot help but wonder how will we be judged in the future.

13. Does Peer Pressure Ever End?

During a school holiday period I spent some time with a niece. She was almost fifteen at the time and during our days together we chatted about a whole range of things; from girlish hair-stuff to some much deeper issues.

Peer pressure was an interesting topic. I had forgotten how hard it is to be a teenager and to perhaps be a little different to many of the girls in the classroom. In many ways peer pressure is just nastiness in its' most unsophisticated form and it can also be equated to bullying.

It is an unfortunate part of growing up but my niece understood that one day it will be over and everybody will be on an equal footing. But then, long after she had returned home I started to think about that .....

Does peer pressure ever end?

The Macquarie Dictionary defines a *peer* as *'an equal in any respect'* and a *peer group* as *'a group of people of the same social background, occupation, or class'*. [5]

Teenagers believe equality is about the way they look, act or dress. They can be cruelly outspoken in their approach to this, causing much grief to those that might not fit the mould. The kids seem to be more materialistic these days and they also seem to have more money, but that is also another topic for another book.

Their parents unconsciously do the same, but peer pressure is not openly spoken about among adults. It is laughingly referred to as "keeping up with the Joneses", and if you look around you can see it everywhere, every day.

Take a drive through some of the newer housing estates. The abundance of affluence is astounding. The sheer size of the houses, as well as those being built, and the accompanying landscaping would have you believe that there are no financial problems in any part of the world at all and certainly not around this neighbourhood.

Have a look at the cars in the parking lot where you shop. How many of them are older than three years? Then ask yourself this question – how many of them were bought without finance? Would a five or seven year old car go just as well as a new one? It probably would, but it just does not look as up-to-the-minute as the new one, does it?

And if you are reading this and thinking it does not apply to you – then go and check your wardrobe. Look at the shoes and the clothes that you have purchased recently. Did you buy them because you needed them, or because what you already have are out dated as last year's fashions? Would trying to keep up with the latest fashions amount to a form of peer pressure?

Because we live in a society where we are told "we can have it all", parents are quick to make sure that not only do they look and possess the same as everyone else, but that their offspring are the same. And it would appear that if needs be, they borrow copious amounts of money to do so.

So while it all might look real, if you are to believe the statistics about the levels of borrowed money in this country, it would seem that the appearances and perception of wealth are only as great as the available balance on the owner's credit cards.

Already there are alarming reports of the huge amounts of credit card debt being racked up by the younger generation. Now where did they get that idea from?

There will always be 'the-haves' and the 'have-nots'. But whilst there continues to be an ever-ready stream of credit available for the taking, peer pressure will continue to thrive.

[5] "peer", "peer group". *MacquarieDictionary.com.au* 2015 http://www.macquariedictionary.com.au (6 October 2015)

14. The Value Of A Coin

Some time ago, I popped into a supermarket to pick up a couple of small but necessary things. The total of my items came to $8.70. As I went to hand over the ten dollar note from my wallet, I became aware of the weight in my purse from all the coins I had accumulated over the week. "Hang on a minute" I said to the girl at the checkout. And I counted out the correct money for my purchases from the coins.

Glancing up, I noticed the expression on the girl's face. It was not a pretty sight. She was obviously not impressed with having to handle the coins and then count them into the money drawer. I can understand that a little because apart from my purse, where else had they been?

But I was a little puzzled by her reaction and as I walked away I began to think in general about our attitudes towards coins and how little importance we place on the humble coin.

For many of us it is the first form of money that we identify with. As a child I remember going to church and my parents giving me a coin to put onto the collection plate as it was passed around. I loved the feel of the money, and the imprint fascinated me.

It is interesting to note that the tooth fairy usually brings coins. Even though inflation seems to have caught up with the practice, I am sure there are not too many notes put into glasses of water as a replacement for a lost tooth. And I have not heard of any incidences where money was transferred into the recipient's account via internet banking for tooth fairies.

For children, coins are an important part of the first lessons about saving money. The banks used to give away money boxes in order to promote savings. They do not seem to do that nowadays which makes me wonder if perhaps they also do not place much emphasis on the humble coin either.

Actually, the last time I went into my bank with a year's worth of coin savings, they wanted to charge me a cash-handling fee to count them; regardless of the fact that I had already counted and bagged the coins into bank money bags.

I can understand how coins could seem to be a nuisance at times. They are not good in our pockets. They weigh them down and tear at the corners of the fabric. Have too many in a purse and it feels like a brick in your hand or bag.

So I wonder what most of us do with these coins. Do we keep them in a jar or a fancy money box? Or do we throw them into the bottom of a drawer. I often find them lurking in the bottom of the washing machine and on the floor of my car.

Gathering them together is a great way to save because even though they tend to be treated as nuisance value, coins are still money and classed as legal tender. You can still pay for something by using coins.

I know one couple who annually pay for a weekend getaway with fifty cent pieces. It takes them a year to collect the coins and I imagine the hoteliers must groan when they see them coming. However, they have never knocked back the money!

While it might be a pain in the butt for the store keeper who has to count them, the humble coin should certainly never be dismissed as an inconvenience. And by the same token, we should never discount their value either.

It was not that long ago that some of these coins lived in our wallets as paper notes.

15. The Truth About Downsizing

Downsizing the family home is a term used by lots of people in my parents' generation and it is now becoming a buzz-word for the Baby Boomers.

So what does that mean? What exactly is downsizing?

Whilst working in real estate, lots of older people told me that the reason they wanted to sell their house was because they "needed to downsize".

At the time I accepted that, but I didn't really understand it. Why on earth would you throw away thirty plus years of memories and collectibles to jam yourself and your dearest possessions into a home that is one third the size, with no room to keep all your familiar things?

It did not make sense to me.

But then when I worked as a mortgage

broker I saw some hidden reasons as to why people have a need to downsize.

My parents' generation and indeed many of the Baby Boomers have never had the opportunity to provide adequately for their retirement. So once they retired, all they had to live on was a government pension. As we know that is barely enough money to provide more than a basic standard of living.

With things being a constant struggle, and the only asset they owned being the family home, it made sense to sell that home and buy something smaller. Thus the term – downsizing

So in doing this, the maintenance costs on a smaller place are less and sometimes the running costs are also smaller. Regardless of where you live, your utilities will be pretty much the same cost as they are now. Unless of course you move to another country.

In the past, selling a larger house and buying a smaller home unit or townhouse would result in a reasonably good-sized chunk of money left over after the sale. This could then supplement the old-age pension and the quality of life for the retired was improved.

But then, there was a boom in the property market. Not only did house prices rise, so too did the prices of townhouses, apartments and home units. The tired and in-need-of-maintenance homes owned by the strapped-for-cash retirees were not fetching as good a price as they had previously.

Their owners just did not have the funds to refurbish and repaint to ensure a better price. And if they did, they possibly would then not have a need to sell. Suddenly, there was not a good-sized chunk of money left over at the end of the sale. There seemed to be no point in downsizing.

Some people decided to continue on the downsize plan. For them it meant that they can live in a smaller and newer house that requires little in maintenance and costs for the rest of their lives.

In some cases, some of them had to take out a mortgage to do this and therefore put their already stretched finances under even more strain.

So where is all this leading? Well, I guess it all comes back to planning; planning now for your retirement and for the major financial decisions you will have to make in the future.

If you are still working and feel that you will have a need to downsize your home, for whatever reason, then perhaps it makes sense to do so before you retire from the workforce. That way at least you will still have a steady income to ease the costs of selling and moving house and also perhaps pay a small mortgage.

Or maybe it would just make sense to start working on a household budget now to ensure that you can live in the future on your retirement money without the need to sell your most loved asset, your home.

16. How To Fit Christmas Into Your Budget

Without a doubt, Christmas is one of the most financially stressful times of the year.

We all know how important it is to not have a financial blow-out, yet every year we hear horror stories about families that suffer terribly as a result of over-spending.

Whilst we all seem to over-eat and drink too much over the holiday season, it is the money carnage that has the biggest impact.

It is a crazy time of year for sure. But before you get too embroiled in all the celebrations, let me take a moment to share some thoughts about the festive season .....

Christmas is just one day of the year.

If Christmas is a time for your family traditions, then now is the time to talk about changing or adding some new ones that will not break anybody's budget. You will possibly find that there are some other family members who are also secretly longing for this to happen.

Perhaps your family would benefit from a Pre-Christmas Planning day which will give everybody a chance to plan for the event properly. Why only get together once a year?

Christmas is a time of sharing.

Not only do we share food and drinks but we also share time with our family. Some do that willingly; some do that because it is expected of them.

It is not always easy to get a family of different personalities together for a day of bonding. There are bound to be some frayed and jagged nerves by the end of the day.

If you are hosting the family Christmas party and will have a house full of guests, then hopefully they will contribute something or share some of the chores. Let's face it – it is no fun cooking for a crowd and then having to wash all the dishes as well.

If this is what usually happens at your place (or wherever you spend Christmas), then maybe it is time to change some of your Christmas traditions. You are probably not the only person who needs to watch their money.

Perhaps your 'traditional dinner' could be divided into parts that each guest could provide (e.g. Somebody brings the turkey / ham, somebody else provides the veggies. The pudding could be supplied by somebody else, and the custard could also be made by another guest. Are you getting the idea here?)

Here are some further tips:

- Consider keeping it simple - you could always arrange for a 'buffet' lunch, where everybody brings a platter.
- If you are cooking lunch at home, delegate tasks. You do not need to do everything yourself.
- Share the cooking – ask guests to participate by contributing a part of the menu. Do not forget that there are other people who would love to bring their 'family favourite'.
- Plan your menu in advance and also use a shopping list.

- Store brands are great for side dishes and salads etc - nobody will even realise!
- And of course, it is not just the food costs that need to be calculated, liquid refreshments also need to be considered. Here are some ideas:
- A lot of money is spent on alcohol at Christmas. Try serving guests a festive glass of punch – you can even stretch out servings with apple juice.
- Christmas punch goes a long way, and is less expensive (alcoholic and non-alcoholic).
- Use lots of ice – this also helps make drinks last longer when the weather is hot.

Christmas is a time of giving.

When it comes to gifts, many of us tend to go overboard in that department. How many times have we heard people tell us that Christmas has become too commercial? Or – "it is the thought that counts" when it comes to gift giving.

Have you ever wondered why so many people seem to place such great importance on the price of the gifts from family members, that they only just tolerate, and hardly see throughout the rest of the year?

We have all heard many times, the complaint – "the stingy so and so only bought me a measly ....."

Of course, from those whom we love unconditionally, we would accept the button off their shirt as a gift – if we knew that was all they could afford.

Maybe in future Christmases we could give an extra gift of tolerance and understanding to those relatives who we find hard to love. It will not cost anything and you may be surprised by the results.

When it comes to buying presents, the first thing to do is to make a list of everybody that you need to buy a Christmas gift for and stick to the list! Then:

- Work out how much you can comfortably afford to spend on each gift, and do not overspend.
- Consider a Kris Kringle (Secret Santa) for large family gift-giving events; where everyone draws a name out of a hat and

buys a present only for that person. (You are not the only one on a budget).

- Choose a theme for your gifts – calendars, books, chocolates, home-made treats, socks, pens, glasses, pillows, etc. This works really well with a Kris Kringle because the focus is then placed on getting the most suitable gift to for each recipient.
- Give vouchers – lawn mowing, painting, baby-sitting, house cleaning etc. Nowadays people are time poor, not possession poor.
- Spending time with loved ones is the best gift of all. Consider a family day pass to the zoo or theme park. Movie tickets for a family outing will also be appreciated
- If you are one of those people that just love to decorate the house to celebrate the season, then you may also need to keep an eye on those costs. Follow these simple steps:
- Do not over-spend on decorations. Recycle the ones from last year or just add one or two new pieces.
- Wrap gifts in bright and glossy junk mail—it all ends up in the same place in the end!
- If you must have Christmas lights all over the place – get solar-powered ones and at least cut down on your electricity costs.

- Buy inexpensive candles and decorate them yourself with a Christmas theme. Use tinsel, glitter and ribbons to decorate and save money instead of buying pre-packaged Christmas ones.
- When decorating the dinner table. Buy inexpensive glasses and paint each guests name on the side, or attach a tag with each name to a glass stem. Use them as an extra gift for everyone, and this also helps with not having heaps of glasses to wash. (Each guest takes their gift-glass home).

For lots of people, spending time with family and loved ones is the best part of Christmas and it is important to remember that the best Christmas memories are about people and events. The size and cost of the gifts are insignificant.

If you have not already done so, it is a good idea to start your Christmas planning early. Doing this will avoid a major 'money melt-down' due to lack of preparation.

Did you know that people who leave everything to the last minute will spend more money because they have run out of time?

So it does not matter how much money you do or do not have, you can fit Christmas into your budget. If you spend more time on the planning, you can make sure you spend less money on the event.

17. How To Save When You Shop

A young mother was telling me about "how much money she had saved" when she was out on a recent shopping trip. It sounded great. She and a girlfriend had spent several hours in the shopping mall looking for bargains – and they had found heaps .....

The first shop they visited was a well-known clothing store that was having a fifty percent discount sale on all items. Both of them spent $120 on clothing which, if there had not been a sale at the time they were shopping, would have cost $240. Happily, she told me that they had been able to buy all the items they wanted for half of the usual price.

Then, they visited a shoe store that was also having a sale and each purchased a new pair of shoes for twenty five percent off the usual price. Of course, no outfit is complete without the right accessories, so the next stop was at the jewelers where they also were offering ten per cent off all their earrings and bracelets.

By this time, they had tried on everything they had looked at, bought their 'to die for' items at bargain prices and were ready for lunch. The local bistro was offering a special price for a glass of wine and a salad and it was the obvious choice for this pair of 'Money Saving Queens'.

Of course, I was suitably impressed and asked just exactly how much they had saved in dollar terms. With a pencil and paper she worked it out for me… one hundred and twenty dollars saved in the clothing store; thirty dollars from the shoe shop and twelve dollars at the jewelers. Add on the seven dollars saved on the lunch deal and it came to a grand total of one hundred and sixty two dollars saved.

When I asked which bank account the money was going in to, my young friend looked puzzled. She did not understand what I meant. But maybe I did not understand what she meant. Because you see, when she told me that she had saved a heap of money I believed that she had been able to make all of these purchases and then put the money she had saved into her savings account.

But that was not the case at all. My friend had only managed to avoid paying the full price for her items. She had not actually saved any money at all.

In fact the advertising and marketing were so good in making her believe that she was saving money, that she spent more than she would have if she had put the first lot of "savings" into the bank. And all the time she was certain that she was 'saving money'.

And therein lies a problem. So many people believe that if they buy an item at a discounted price then they are saving money. But unless they put the actual monetary difference between the usual price and the discount price into a savings account, then they are not saving anything. They are just not paying full price.

I guess a lot of this has to do with terminology and the stories that we tell ourselves. With the help of todays' clever marketing strategies, we can convince ourselves that if we pay fifty dollars less for an item then we are saving money.

This is possibly the reason why todays' society seems to equate the word saving to mean 'discount'. And if the word discount means to reduce, then is it any wonder that our savings accounts are dwindling?

And that is just another reason why our budgets are up the proverbial creek without a paddle!

18. Talking About Money

I often get asked this question – "Is it bad manners to discuss money with people?"

Now, I know there is a school of thought that says one should not ever discuss 'sex, religion or politics.' Sometimes it would seem that the topic of money is included in that as well. Because it is a topic that people just do not talk about. It is almost like a social taboo but therein lies one of the problems that face our society.

Because nobody talks about money there are many people that base their opinions and sometimes facts on assumptions and perceptions. Which brings me to another point – if I had a dollar for every time that I have heard the expression "I have got wealthy friends" then I'm sure I would be wealthy too.

Sadly, the fact of the matter is that we just do not ever discuss money – not with our families and certainly not amongst our friends. What this leads to is that many people have no commonsense financial literacy and are therefore easy prey for all sorts of unscrupulous get-rich-quick money deals.

For some people, the only time they ever hear anybody discussing money (and how to make it etc) is when they have been coerced into one of those 'retire early' type seminars run by 'spruikers'. And then, because these fast talking types appear to make sense (and they probably would if you had never heard this type of sales-pitch before) the poor innocents get caught up and are led along like lambs to the slaughter. They lose their money, their pride and any hope of an open discussion about money is now gone!

Like many people, growing up in a family where there was not a lot of money meant that if we ever discussed the topic, it was probably more along the lines of how to make it, rather than how to save it or even how to manage it.

When times were tough (and that was most of the time), the easy answer to a request for something was "No, I don't have any money". As children, we learned to accept that response and we also learned the value of rare treats.

Money was something that did not get squandered.

But whilst we learned a healthy respect for the commodity we did not really ever discuss money.

When was the last time you sat around at a barbecue and seriously talked about your mortgage, or the level of your debt? Well you probably have not ever done this and you cannot imagine ever doing that either. And there is a part of me that suddenly feels that I have just got myself taken off the invitation lists of all the parties that are coming up.

Of course, there is always a time and a place for a personal money discussion and there are a lot of social events where it is certainly not a good idea to initiate such a subject. But if you do not ever have this conversation – then how the hell are you going to learn anything about the topic?

19. Why People Shun Budgets

Have you ever wondered why so many people shun the thought of using a budget? I had often wondered until one day I had a revelation.

I was reading an email from a budgeting software company that was explaining in a long and drawn out fashion, how to work out a budget. There was nothing exciting in that.

And the whole purpose of the exercise was to show how hard it was to work out a family budget with a pencil and paper. And truly, looking at the explanation, it was hard.

Of course, if you purchased their budgeting software, you could avoid the tedium of such a long winded process.

I have often wondered why it is that so many people I meet have bought such programs only to have them sit virtually untouched in the packaging they came in. Some of them have been opened and some of them have been attempted. But I am yet to see one of these programs up and running successfully. That is, apart from the videos that the creator of the program shows you online.

Now, I am not saying that these programs are crappy. Anything that can help you to learn how to budget has to be good. But it has to be realistic and simple. And it has to make somebody want to adopt it like a second skin, because it is easy.

This made me realise that the major reason people who use my system have such fabulous results, is because they can understand how it works – without having to consult a computer program or a spreadsheet. They just 'get it'.

Apart from the fact that I personally speak to them, and teach them how to set up their own budget, the main difference is that they know exactly the moment when they have overspent on their budget. There is no waiting for a bank statement to tell them; there is no consulting the 'spreadsheet' to see if they have blown it. They know almost instantly.

But none of that was the revelation.

What suddenly hit me was that most 'budgeting systems' are based on, and want you to make, calculations and projections for the coming year. They need you to know in advance how you are going to live your life. And that is generally unrealistic.

Why? Well that is because we all get paid weekly, fortnightly or monthly. None of us get paid on an annual basis. And none of us can accurately predict either our annual income or our annual expenditure.

Sure, we might have a fair idea of these figures. But life is not like that. It is just not that predictable. Let me explain .....

Unless you have a 'fixed rate' on your mortgage, you cannot apportion the annual interest costs of your mortgage, because variable interest rates are subject to fluctuations.

How can you foresee the costs of your utilities when your usage may change because of a change in circumstances? A simpler example of this is that you might decide to purchase a big plasma TV, which are known to use more electricity. Or you might get rid of your vintage refrigerator for a newer model that uses less electricity.

What you spent last year on haircuts, clothes or car costs can change dramatically if you decide to change your hair style, your dress size or perhaps the way you use your car.

A household budget simply cannot run on the annual figures that you forecast on any one particular day. Unless you have a crystal ball, it is just not possible to accurately predict your financial requirements in the future.

The other part of the revelation is this – these 'other' types of budgeting systems are locking you in to living your life the same way, every day, for at least the next year. That is the way they're designed!

And that is so boring!

How lifeless would it be to have to live your life according to the figures that are predicted and set down on paper, one year in advance? There is no room for spontaneity, no money for impromptu excitement, and nothing to look forward to.

That is why so many people shun the idea of having a budget.

I would not like having to live that way, and I would not expect you to, either. But if I could show you a different way – would you be prepared to try it for a month?

20. A Truth About Loyalty Cards

Nowadays it is very common for companies to offer loyalty rewards for their customers. Sometimes it seems that every store you enter is offering bargain prices or other sorts of special offers, just for those people who belong to a loyal customer scheme.

But who is this loyal customer and what is a loyalty reward? And at what price does this reward come?

If the dictionary defines *loyalty* as *'faithful adherence to a sovereign or government, or to a leader, cause, or the like'* [6] then in this instance it means that either the customer will only ever shop in that place, or the company will always reward returning customers. And it seems, that you only have to sign up and you are automatically into the program.

One of our major retail stores automatically gives me a discount every time I shop there. I have never asked for it, nor signed anything. They tell me it is because I have "shopped there before and that means I am a loyal customer".

But I have a "best price on the day" policy when I shop for the type of items that they sell. If I end up purchasing from them it does not necessarily mean that I am being loyal. It means that they have the best price for the item.

They do not provide a store loyalty card and I often wonder why they do not just lower the prices of all their stock by the ten per cent that they so readily seem to give everybody who is loyal.

Some of the more well-known loyalty cards are provided by the airlines. If you travel a lot, it is a great way to get discounted seats. In the race to get more people in the air, some airlines have even made provision to link your credit card to their loyalty card, thus allowing you to earn more points.

Being a regular traveler, I belong to three Frequent Flyer programs. I have found that regardless of the company I fly with, the points and/or flights all add up to about the same reward ratio which is one in ten flights are free.

Of course, in Australia you can also link your supermarket loyalty card to one of the airline loyalty programs. But have you realised that on a 'one dollar spent for one point rewarded' basis you will need to spend about eight thousand dollars in groceries before being eligible for a flight between a regional city and the capital city of that particular state?

Of course not everything is free. There are loyalty programs that ask you to pay a fee to join. (Huh? They want us to pay them to show that we are loyal?) Sometimes you will need to do your sums carefully before buying this type of rewards program.

If you have a credit card that offers a loyalty rewards program then you should be familiar with the annual fee that you pay in order to accumulate those rewards. Once again, while it is nice to accumulate your points, you also have to calculate the true cost of the reward in real money terms.

One card that I know well, rewards me with one point for every dollar that I spend. Sound great? Well yes, when I have around fifteen thousand reward points – I can get a toaster.

Effectively that means I have spent fifteen thousand dollars before being rewarded with the toaster. Now, with the annual fee being only forty-eight dollars I am beginning to think that maybe I could just keep that money and buy my toaster sooner.

In this day and age while commercial competition is enormous, we are able to make our money stretch further than ever. We would therefore be crazy to pledge allegiance to one particular store or company.

But we can participate in all the free loyalty schemes available. By keeping our wits about us; we can get some truly great discounts along the way!

[6] "loyalty". *MacquarieDictionary.com.au* 2015 http://www.macquariedictionary.com.au (6 October 2015)

21. The Seven Deadly Budget Sins

Which of the Seven Deadly Budget Sins are you currently committing?

1. **Lust.** Being focused on short term profits, being distracted by opportunities that do not add to your overall outcome, not having an outcome. Getting caught up in a frenzy of impulse buying and buying things you do not need or want, just to be able to show your possession status

2. **Gluttony.** Trading your time for money, working in excess of fifty five hours a week. Preferring to rack up debt on credit rather than saving for the things that you want.

3. **Greed.** Focusing on owning possessions instead of cost and value. Wanting everything NOW despite the cost and not being prepared to wait till you can afford it.

4. **Pride.** Believing that you can afford everything and that you have no need to budget. Choosing to 'not worry' about the

future.

5. Sloth. Being lazy about saving for the future.

6. Envy. Wanting to buy everything that others have, not considering the ramifications of collaborating with those around you. Believing the fallacy that says "you can have it all". Forever envying your friends assets.

7. Wrath. Hating your budget and deliberately not making it work. Blaming everybody but yourself for your poor financial situation.

22. Some Thoughts About Shopping

Aaaahhh! Shopping!

The Macquarie Dictionary defines *shopping* as *'the act of someone who shops'* and *shopping* as *'to set out on a shopping expedition'* [7]

What a loaded word it is. It means so many things to so many people. For some it is the ultimate pleasure. Others find it to be a necessary evil.

There are people who find shopping to be a wonderful pastime. They can spend hours and hours browsing the shops, looking for who knows what. Many times they cannot remember what it is that sent them out to forage and hunt – they just do it. And all the while they are enjoying the activity as much as the sports fan who likes to go to the football, or the bookworm who enjoys a visit to the library.

It makes me wonder why some people like

to shop while others do not. In many cases it is the female of our species that seems to enjoy this pursuit as a pleasurable experience. Have a look around the shopping mall and count how many men are sitting on the seats reading a newspaper. They appear to be so patient, waiting for their female partner who is browsing the nearby stores. (Yes, yes, I can hear you saying – "if you only knew").

I am also curious about the belief that 'women are born with a shopping gene'. If that is really the case, then I surely missed out. My mother and sisters all love to shop and their idea of a great 'girls day out' always includes some time at a shopping mall. And when they are traveling – they make sure to visit all the shops, regardless of the fact that many of them are exactly the same as the ones at home.

You should have seen them when we went to Hong Kong! It was at that point in my life that I truly began to question if I had been adopted at birth. Surely I could not have been related to these women who insisted on visiting every single shop that was there? I don't think we missed any of them. And to top it off, we almost missed the plane home because I could not get them out of the shops in the airport terminal. The doors were shut behind us as we rushed aboard the aircraft.

Regardless of whether you are a 'shopaholic' or not – here are a couple of tips from my book – *Money Tips from the Budget Bitch* [8] to give you something to think about when you are next having a shopping trip –

8. Don't go shopping to cheer yourself up when you're feeling miserable.

Yes, I know… all the self-help books tell you to "buy yourself something nice" when you're feeling down in the dumps. Well goodness me - there must be thousands of people out there feeling miserable every day. How much more miserable will you feel when you see the credit card statement at the end of the month?

You don't have to go shopping. There are plenty of other things you can do. Try taking a walk, riding a bike, flying a kite. Perhaps you could try reading a book, doing some gardening, or maybe even just talking to somebody.

'Getting out of the house' doesn't mean you have to go shopping.

Make a list of all the things you would like to do, rather than all the things you would like to buy.

11. Don't use window-shopping as a regular form of entertainment.

This will leave you feeling dissatisfied with your life and all that you have. You will begin to 'want more than you can afford'. Sure, it might not cost anything to window-shop at this point in time, but the long-term costs can be horrendous.

There are many other forms of entertainment that cost the same in the short term but which have much more positive long-term benefits.

Whatever you feel about shopping ….. When it comes time for your next shopping trip - I wish all you shopaholics a happy time and for the others like myself – happy endurance test!

[7] "shopping", "shopping". *MacquarieDictionary.com.au* 2015

http://www.macquariedictionary.com.au (6 October 2015)

[8] Carmel McCartin, *Money Tips from the Budget Bitch; The Book of Don'ts*, Budget Bitch Pty Ltd, Thurgoona, NSW, 2013, pp 15, 21

23. Sustainability Is Not New

Isn't it amazing how much everybody and everything is focused on sustainability these days? And while that is a good thing too, it is not new!

To all those people who believe that they have discovered sustainability and saving the planet (amongst other sorts of savings), then I have to say – you are not the first!

Your grandparents and or great grandparents have always been way ahead of you. It is just that nobody stopped to listen to them.

You see, the older generation who has sometimes been called Generation G (generation grandparents) understands saving and sustainability much more than Generation X, Y & Z ever will. For these people who lived through or were born immediately after an economic depression, sustainability and savings are almost second nature.

Drive through any suburb after dark and I will

bet you can pick the houses that belong to Generation G because they are the ones that do not have all the lights blazing in every room. They have always turned off lights in rooms that are not being used.

Ask your grandparents or great grandparents how often they use their electric blankets and they will laugh at you. For them, there's nothing wrong with a good old hot water bottle and a couple of extra blankets on those cold and frosty nights.

While the young people of today look for central heating, their grandparents block off areas of their house and only heat one room at a time (the one they are using), thus making huge savings in greenhouse emissions and keeping money in their wallets.

Have a peek over the back fence and you will possibly see a well-tended vegetable garden. These people have known the value of having home-grown food long before it became fashionable to 'eat local'.

And speaking of food – grandmas and grandpas know how to cook and they do it regularly. They are also well known for baking biscuits, cakes and other goodies which help to make them sustainable by contributing to their savings. You will not find them buying their lunch or paying $7 for a slice of cake every day.

Suggest to your grandparents that re-using water is a good idea and you will find that they can tell you ways that you have never heard of. They have probably always re-cycled the washing machine water and the bucket in the shower certainly is not a new idea. How else do they manage to have such wonderful gardens?

Clothes may have become cheaper and socks cheap enough to almost be disposable, but Generation G has spent many hours sewing and repairing their old ones. A young person of today would have no idea what darning entails, if they have even heard the word. They probably spend hundreds of dollars replacing instead of repairing.

So for those people who think that the whole sustainable savings thing is brand new – think again. These very senior citizens have always known about savings, but they call it "common sense".

As these people turn eighty, ninety, one hundred and more, ask yourself how they managed to live that long? Is there a secret? Maybe not. And just think about this fact – if they lived their lives the way some of us do, they would not be the age they are now.

Surely we can understand that Generation G have a wealth of practices and experiences that can make not only ourselves but our planet sustainable for many centuries to come?

We might not always have agreed with what they have told us in the past and we have probably fobbed them off as being 'old fuddy duddies'. But if we want to learn some valuable lessons for our future then we only have to start listening to them.

24. The Bag Of Christmas Cheer

Imagine this scenario – the date is early December and you are away from home, staying in a hotel. Your brother (who lives nearby) calls and invites you to join his family for their Christmas celebration. All their family will be together this weekend, so they are celebrating early. Being a part of their family, they would love you to come. Its just twenty four hours away.

My brother has five kids who are all grown and they all have partners; there are also some grandkids plus other extended family members. The total is twenty, and there will be an exchange of gifts at some point during the day.

Now this is not part of my Christmas plans and I am totally unprepared to partake in the gift giving ritual. If there had been more time, I would have been able to put some extra money aside throughout the year. I would also have had time to organise something special for each of them.

So here I am, twenty four hours to prepare and not only is there a shortage of funds but I am also lacking inspiration in the gift buying department. When I think about it, even twenty tins of biscuits is going to cost more than one hundred dollars.

And then at 2am it hit me! The answer came from my subconscious while I slept. I knew exactly what to do.

The earliest I could get to the shopping mall was lunch time. And I quickly found a large 'discount' shop. So far so good!

Grabbing a shopping basket, I began the next part of my mission – to buy twenty gifts at a cost of no more than two dollars each. Nothing should be too obviously gender-specific; but to liven the party I chose some purely male and female gifts. (Men's razors, girly soaps; that sort of thing).

I helped myself to the pile of free store catalogues to use as wrapping paper, (they are colourful and end up in the same place as gift wrap), then spent two dollars for a large festive paper bag to carry everything. Back at the hotel I borrowed scissors and sticky-tape from the reception desk and soon everything was wrapped.

Family gatherings are great fun and this was no exception. The joy of spending time with people I love, but am separated from by time and distance, was immeasurable. Just to be with them was my own personal Christmas treat.

And then it was time for the gifts. My brother took me aside, quietly apologised for the short notice and explained that nobody would be upset that I had nothing for them all. Just being together would be enough.

He was right, being together was fabulous, but I was ready to surprise them. When all the presents had been opened, there remained under the tree, a large bag that nobody had seen before.

With a flourish I announced that it was time for "Aunty Carmel's Bag of Christmas Cheer". Everybody would get a lucky-dip and if they did not like their gift – too bad. They could always exchange with somebody else later.

What a hoot! We played a trivia game with a dip into the bag being the prize; everybody was a winner. An hour later, we were still laughing and swapping gifts. Even Grandma got into the spirit, swapping screwdrivers for incense sticks.

It was the best forty-two dollars I have ever spent and it is a new tradition; with family members competing to prove their need to be named as the Christmas Cheer Bag person.

You know, sometimes I think we have forgotten that Christmas memories are about people and events. The size and cost of the gifts are insignificant.

25. What Does It Cost To Have Fun?

Let me ask you a question – if you won a million dollars, what would you do with it?

You will probably tell me that you will buy a house (if you don't already have one) or perhaps you will pay off your mortgage and you will possibly be able to clear all your debt.

Of course, you will have to have a party to celebrate, and you might give a share of your winnings to family and friends.

A million dollars does not seem to go too far these days, depending on how much debt you have to get rid of and what you want to buy. But whatever you decide to do, I am sure the main focus will be to have fun. (At least while the money lasts).

Now, imagine for a moment that you did not win and you do not have a million dollars. For most of us, that is not terribly hard to imagine. We are as close to having a million dollars in the bank as we are to the moon. (Although did you know that in Australia, in our working lifetimes we earn, on average, four million dollars each?)

So if we do not have all that money in ready cash, how do we have fun? Sitting here at my desk, I shudder to think what the answers will be.

And I will bet that you are all thinking that just because I am a Budget Bitch, I do not believe in fun. But I do ,enormous loads of it, and it does not have to cost a lot of money either.

For those of you that cannot imagine how to have fun without blowing the budget, let me help with just a few ideas .....

- A picnic in the park does not cost much – just some sandwiches and drinks, with perhaps a Frisbee or a bat and ball for amusement.
- A visit to the library – there are heaps of great things to do there. I am not going to tell you what they are. You need to go find out for yourself!

- If you cannot afford the cheap cinema prices on Tuesdays, hire a DVD and snuggle up on the couch.
- Kite flying is great on a windy day. You can make the kites yourself and spend even less money.
- Board games are a great investment and a lot of fun.
- Rent toys instead of buying them, or join a toy library.
- Go to the beach. One of the most wonderfully entertaining places in the world is absolutely free. You can get almost the same buzz from sitting on the bank of a lake or river.
- Plan a meal, invite your friends over and ask them to not only bring some of the ingredients, but ask them to help with the cooking. It is a very social activity, and can be loads of fun. (barbecues and salads in Summer, one-pot meals in Winter)
- Organise a hand-me-down party with your friends, and set a theme such as kids clothes, kids toys, household goods etc. (this is a party-plan with a difference).
- Go for a walk and make sure you talk to at least 10 people. Even saying hello is better than looking away.

See? You do not need a million dollars to have a good time. You do not need very much money at all really and I am sure that you could come up with at least another ten good ideas that will not cost a lot of money.

When you really think about it, much of the time "having a good time" is simply just a state of mind.

26. Some Things Stay The Same

The internet in Australia has been around commercially for about twenty years at the time of writing. That is not very long if you are talking to a Baby Boomer. And it is the mere blink of an eye to somebody who is an octogenarian or older.

But what it does mean is that anybody born after 1995 will have grown up with this medium. Unlike their older counterparts, these young people are not in awe of this technology because it has been around for as long as they can remember.

Is it not funny though, how these kids are expected to know how it all works? Unlike their parents and grandparents, this young generation just accepts and uses the technology every day without giving it much thought. They are not interested in knowing about the ins and outs of the computer. They do not have a need to know how it all works.

If something goes wrong, they get a

repairman to fix it. One young nephew explained it to me by saying "I don't have to understand how it all works; I just use it and make it work for me."

I guess it was the same in the early 1900's when cars and telephones were invented. At the time it probably took a while for the general public to embrace the technology and I am sure there were many sceptical opinions being voiced. But just look how far we have come since then.

The world became a smaller place with the advent of not only these things but also with wireless and television transmissions. Suddenly, we were able to communicate and associate with people from far away; not just across town but all over the world.

If you speculate about the future, you should be able to see that our world will probably work quite amicably with an online community for business and pleasure as well as the traditional face to face relationships. For the older generations it seems strange, but future generations will not know any different.

Whether you like it or not – if you are a business person, you will need to get in touch with the capabilities of the internet unless you want to be left behind. That does not mean everything will be done that way, but already we are seeing banking, retail, wholesale, and social transactions taking place in this medium.

Sometimes nowadays it seems like there is nothing that cannot be converted into a computer program. Recently I had an aspiring young chap tell me that I need to embrace technology and sell budget planning via the internet. He assured me that together, with his help, we could make a substantial profit from an impressive program that he has invented.

But let me tell you this:

You can chase the figures around and around using all sorts of clever computer programs and spreadsheets. You can make all the figures and projections look very fancy with all manner of colourful pie-charts and graphs. You can give it all a fancy name.

But the simple fact of the matter is this, a budget remains as the most basic financial plan that every single person needs to manage their money. And you do not need this new technology to work one out.

Whether we like it or not, computers and the internet are definitely here to stay.

Regardless of how it all pans out in the future there a couple of things that I know for certain will never change:

1. The sun will continue to rise in the east and set in the west. Every day.

2. If you spend more than you earn, you will get yourself into trouble.

27. The Image Obsession

Have you noticed how it seems that as a society we have become obsessed with self-image? I mean, seriously, take a good look around you and you will see what I mean.

We can start with the houses in our streets. Why do we seem to be obsessed with having the biggest and latest look in construction? If you live in an older suburb, have you noticed how many places are either upgraded in space and design or have been completely pulled down to make way for a much larger, more modern building.

And when it comes to buying houses, I ask why a young newly married couple would need a house with four or five bedrooms. Could it mean that they have already decided to sleep alone in separate rooms? Or is it because it gives them bragging rights in the 'Who has the biggest mortgage stakes'?

If the statistics showing that the average person lives in their house for only seven years are true, then buying what we need now would possibly be a sensible approach. There are not too many newlyweds these days that can or even want to fill such huge houses within the space of seven years.

When it comes to our gardens every bush and blade of grass is trimmed within a centimetre of perfection. And if we cannot do it for ourselves, there is a huge industry of gardeners who are available to give that flawless look to the exterior of our homes.

I often wonder why somebody with only a seven hundred square metre block of land would need a ride-on mower. I can understand if it is because they have got a problem with their legs, cannot walk, and therefore might not be able to push a mower. But I also wonder if it is an image thing?

Or maybe it is to save some time so that they can head down to the gym for a fitness work-out?

And there is another thing; we are so obsessed with losing weight and having a 'hot body' that we are literally spending thousands of dollars each year to ensure that we can still fit into our wedding attire from twenty-five or more years ago. Surely every bump, lump and wrinkle tells a story that we should be proud to share.

The cosmetics industry is making millions from our self-image obsession. And it is not just women who are spending up big to make themselves look as unblemished as, if not better than, everybody else. Men too are now spending huge sums for primping and preening their image in an attempt at outer perfection.

Have you noticed how we are obsessed with having the biggest and smartest car? Why else would there be so many brand new SUVs in the parking lot. Do we really need them? Do we have to drive across great lengths of dirt roads, filled with pot holes and ruts every day? Judging from the lack of dirt on these vehicles, I would say the answer is no.

Maybe there really is some truth to the rumour that we spend too much of our money to impress people that we don't even know or like. Some statistics are showing that seventy five per cent of the money we spend is being spent on our image. That does not leave much for the necessities in life, does it?

Competition is healthy, but sometimes I think we have gone a little too far in 'being the best'.

And whilst some people foolishly spout the belief that 'nothing succeeds like excess' even Donald Trump has been known to say "A little more moderation would be good" [9].

[9]. Trump, Donald. "Donald Trump Quotes" *Brainy Quote.com,* http://www.brainyquote.com/quotes/quotes/d/donaldtrum130904.html (7 October 2015)

28. When Do You Become An Adult?

It is often suggested to me that budgeting should be taught within the education system. However, I tend to believe that budgeting is a life skill rather than a school subject and these skills are usually learned at home.

I was asked to speak to a high school class about money and budgets with a bit of common sense thrown in as well. These kids were old enough to legally leave school and start work.

Most people tell me that kids need to learn how to budget their pocket money, but many of these were already working part time jobs and earning substantially more than pocket money. They were preparing for the time when they leave school, move out of home and become responsible for themselves.

So what would you talk to these high school kids about? Well, once they leave school and start work, regardless of their age, they have become young adults. I asked the obvious question, "what does being an adult mean?"

I was pleasantly surprised. Most of these kids have definitely got a handle on what it is all about. In lots of ways, they seemed to have more idea than some older people that I know.

They cited the major attribute of an adult was being responsible. I have to admit that I thought it would take a while to get this answer, but these kids certainly realised this is a major part of being grown-up. Chalk one up for the youth of today!

So then we discussed responsibility and they listed all the areas where they would need to be responsible; for themselves, their actions, their money and then ultimately a family of their own.

In the money section, they all agreed that too much debt was not good and that paying your bills on time was important. But they did not have much of an idea of how to make their money last till the next pay day.

I was not surprised; as many parents possibly have no idea either. They had all heard the word budget, but did not really know what it meant. They tended to regard the topic like a visit to the dentist where you just do the bare minimum and then worry when it hurts.

Using an example of moving out of home, we created a fictitious budget. They all had a fair idea of what rent would cost and what bills they might have to pay. Yet, they had never before thought to add up the costs.

We included the running expenses of the car they decided that they had to have, threw in a couple of their usual night out costs and suddenly they were needing to earn an income of fifty thousand dollars a year.

It was all looking a little grim, till they decided how to reduce some costs: Walking or riding a bike could cut the transport costs, entertain at home; cooking rather than buying take-away. These kids were starting to think very responsibly.

They decided that living at home was an alternative option and they agreed that paying their way was also a responsible adult thing to do.

And then it all got too much for one young chap. He threw his arms into the air and declared "I don't care what you say! It has nothing to do with money! If you have left school and you feel like an adult, then you are an adult".

I had no choice. In light of what we had just spent the past two hours discussing, I had to say "Honey, if you are over twenty-one with a full time job and you are living with your parents, that is OK. You can feel whichever way you want to feel. But if you are not paying your way and your mother is still buying your deodorant and your underpants – then you are not an adult!"

And with that – the class disintegrated!

29. Are Your Finances Apple Or Pear Shaped?

The end of the financial year is always a great time to take stock of the promises we made to ourselves when the year had just started. Are we on track to achieve what we wanted for this year? Are we making a little progress at least? Or have we not started as yet?

It is also at that time of year that our thoughts turn to the shape of our finances. Are they shiny and bright like a crisp new apple? Or have they gone a little 'pear-shaped'?

It does not seem to be easy to make ends meet for a lot of people at times - money doesn't seem to stretch as far at the supermarket; car, health and household insurances go up again; council rates and taxes always seem to be on the increase and electricity prices rise more often than many of us expect.

At those times it seems like our wallets are being attacked from all sides. I guess you don't need anyone to remind you just how tough it can get.

The end of the financial year is also the time when we gather together all our paperwork and receipts in preparation for filing our tax return. It is traditionally the time when a lot of financial decisions are made or re-evaluated.

If you are a 'pay as you go' (PAYG) employee then it is also the time of year when you will receive your payment summary and prepare to submit your annual returns to the Taxation Office.

There are many ways to get the paperwork done – you can do it yourself by filling in the paper forms and posting them in; or by going online you can fill in the information using the appropriate forms from the Australian Taxation Office website and lodge it electronically.

There are also tax agents and accountants who are more than willing to do this task for you, and in many cases you can claim their fee as a legitimate tax deduction next year.

Using a tax professional can save you the worry of keeping up with the changing rules about deductions and in many cases they can also assist with getting you a higher refund than you might have expected if you are battling with the paperwork yourself.

If you are fortunate enough to be getting a refund, there is always the question of what to do with it. Is it for spending or saving?

Of course, what many people fail to realise is that this money is actually a part of their income. It was just paid to the Taxation Office in advance, to ensure your tax obligations were met. So if you are one of those people who regularly use their credit card as an extension of their wages – tax refund time is the perfect time to repay that debt.

If your credit card balance is cleared every month, your tax refund could be used to help reduce your mortgage. This in turn will lower the interest payable (as it is calculated daily on the balance of what you owe) and will help to get your property paid off a little faster. Sounds tempting, does it not?

Of course, if you are fortunate enough to be in the small minority of people that have no debt, then you get to make the decision as to whether you spend the money or save it.

Perhaps you consider this money to be a non-conventional form of saving and you have already chosen to purchase something that you have been saving for. You might have enough to get that TV you have wanted, or perhaps a holiday is in order.

But let me ask just one question before you sail off to the shops. If your hot water system dies tomorrow, do you already have enough money saved to replace it? Without needing to borrow the money or use any form of credit?

These days it is no longer considered unfashionable to have a savings account and there are plenty of long and short term savings options available, if that is what you have decided to do with the money.

Putting some money away for your long term future is a great idea, but it is also important to have a back-up plan to pay for any unexpected expenses when they occur.

Regardless of what you decide, for every person and/or household that has an income now is the time to assess your money and how you're managing.

If you have fallen behind in your savings plan – then now is the time to make amends. If you're falling behind in paying your bills when they're due – then now is the time to organise or re-organise your budget.

30. What Lesson Will They Learn?

"On the advice of our financial planner, when our child was born we set up a 'strictly no touching' savings account with the funds to be given to him or her when they turn eighteen."

How many of you have been given the same advice?

But I do not understand how some parents can religiously contribute to their kids' savings accounts and never touch the money – yet at the same time are unable to save anything for themselves.

I was called to see a young couple who were having trouble making ends meet and were in fear of the bank repossessing their home. They had not been married very long, had a two year old child and were expecting another baby within a week or two.

Money-wise, with only one income, things were really tight. Apart from their mortgage which was consuming a large portion of their income, they had no other loans.

But with the husbands work hours being cut back, winter ills and the associated costs of the imminent new baby, they had been so busy juggling things that they had not only gotten behind with their bills; they had also missed some mortgage payments.

Both parents looked pale and seemed fragile. Further questioning confirmed my suspicions – they were not eating every day. They did say, however, that their little child ate well every day.

Together we started to add up some figures. Boy! There was not much money coming in and I could certainly see why they juggled their funds all the time. Then I asked about the Family Allowance from the government; were they receiving it?

Oh yes, they assured me, they were getting it and were putting it into a bank account each fortnight; a bank account for their son, that they wouldn't touch. And they were very proud of the fact that he now had a little over seven thousand dollars in savings.

Oh dear! These people were in serious danger of becoming homeless and their toddler was financially secure enough to leave home and set himself up in a rental property. I think he was the wealthiest two year old I had ever met.

This is not an isolated story. Nowadays we seem to have lots of pre-schoolers with bank accounts containing hundreds and sometimes thousands of dollars – yet their parents are struggling to keep the roof over their head, and food on the table.

And in many cases not only do their parents have no savings of their own but they are using their credit cards each week as an extension of their salary. In many cases, they do this just to 'get by'. Just imagine the stress this causes!

How do we explain to these young people that Family Allowance is money provided by the government to assist with feeding, clothing and educating their children? How can we get them to see that growing up in a safe home with happy parents is more important than a fistful of dollars when their kids leave school?

And how do we get them to understand that they are teaching a lesson to their children about saving for others, but not for themselves.

The gift of saving is perhaps the greatest lesson you can give your child. The lessons you teach them will possibly last longer than the money you save in an account for them. While the end result may be wonderful, it is the journey that they will always remember.

While it might be nice to hand them twenty thousand dollars when they arrive into adulthood, the value will always be somewhat diminished if they do not understand the importance of saving.

Is it fair to present them with an end result if they have not taken part in the journey?

ABOUT THE AUTHOR

Carmel McCartin is an accomplished writer and speaker. Her articles have been published both online and in the print media. This is her fifth book.

She established the Budget Bitch company in 2007 after two years research whilst working as a personal budget consultant. She is a regular commentator for local and current budgeting issues.

In Australia she is known as #1*Budget Guru* and has assisted numerous clients get their finances back on track.

This book is all about common sense ideas that can be applied to anybody's personal situation.

You will find all her books here www.amazon.com/author/carmelmccartin.